THE MLB FAN'S GUIDE

12 REASONS TO LOVE THE LOS ANGELES ANGELS

by Doug Williams

12 STORY LIBRARY

www.12StoryLibrary.com

12-Story Library is an imprint of Peterson Publishing Company and Press Room Editions.

Produced for 12-Story Library by Red Line Editorial

Photographs ©: John Cordes/Icon Sportswire/AP Images, cover, 1, 23; Gary Stewart/AP Images, 5; Matty Zimmerman/AP Images, 6; AP Images, 7; Bettmann/Corbis, 9; Neal Preston/Corbis, 10; Lennox McLendon/AP Images, 12; Dennis Cook/AP Images, 13; Kevork Djansezian/AP Images, 14; Jim Cowsert/AP Images, 15; Eric Risberg/AP Images, 16; Reed Saxon/AP Images, 18; Jae C. Hong/AP Images, 21; Peter Joneleit/Cal Sport Media/AP Images, 22, 28; The Jon B. Lovelace Collection of California Photographs/Carol M. Highsmith's America Project/Library of Congress, 24; Ffooter/Shutterstock Images, 25, 29; Kelly Nash/Rex Features/AP Images, 26

ISBN
978-1-63235-212-5 (hardcover)
978-1-63235-239-2 (paperback)
978-1-62143-264-7 (hosted ebook)

Library of Congress Control Number: 2015934317

Printed in the United States of America
Mankato, MN
October, 2015

TABLE OF CONTENTS

1

THE COWBOY GETS A TEAM

As a boy in Oklahoma, Gene Autry loved playing baseball, even if he wasn't the greatest player. "I was always a frustrated ballplayer," he once said. Instead of playing ball as an adult, Autry became an actor, singer, and businessman. He gained fame as a singing cowboy in movies of the 1930s and 1940s.

Yet Autry never stopped loving baseball. So in 1960, when the American League (AL) announced it would add two teams, Autry put together a group to buy one of them. The group paid $2.45 million for the expansion team. The team was named the Los Angeles Angels. A minor league team of the same name had played in Los Angeles from 1903 to 1957.

Autry owned the team for 38 years. He was known to fans as "The Cowboy." Players admired him for his love of the game. His team played in Los Angeles from 1961 to 1965. Autry then moved the team to Anaheim for the 1966 season. He changed the team's name to the California Angels.

For years, the Angels had little success. But in the 1970s and 1980s, Autry paid big money to a number of top free agents. He brought in star sluggers, such as Reggie Jackson, Joe Rudi, and Don Baylor.

The strategy worked. The Angels reached the playoffs for the first time in 1979. Then they did so again in 1982 and 1986. But as long as Autry owned the team, the Angels never reached the World Series.

"Baseball has been the most exciting and frustrating experience of my life," he said. "In the movies, I never lost a fight. In baseball, I hardly ever won one."

Gene Autry visits the Angels' spring training in 1993.

26

Jersey number the Angels retired to honor Gene Autry in 1982.

- Major League Baseball (MLB) teams have 25 players.
- Autry was the Angels' honorary 26th player.

2

THE ANGELS TAKE FLIGHT

Expansion teams typically start with a lot of players other teams didn't want. So the first Los Angeles Angels team in 1961 was an odd mix of old stars and rookies. The AL season is 162 games. Some experts predicted the team wouldn't win 50 of them.

The Angels had aging veterans. Relief pitcher Ryne Duren had been an All-Star for the New York Yankees. First baseman Ted Kluszewski had been a great power hitter for the Cincinnati Reds. Third baseman Eddie Yost had many serviceable years for the Washington Senators. But all were at least 32 years old in 1961. Kluszewski was in his final season at age 36.

The veterans were thrown together with rookies, such as pitcher Dean Chance, catcher Bob Rodgers, and shortstop Jim Fregosi.

The Angels' Del Rice slides safely into home in a 1961 game against the New York Yankees.

86

Surprising victory total by the Angels in 1962.

- The Angels were in first place on the Fourth of July.
- They finished the season third in the AL.

Angels slugger Ted Kluszewski in 1961

"We had a bunch of guys that no one else wanted," said first baseman Lee Thomas. Yet from their first game on April 11 in Baltimore, the Angels were full of surprises. In that game, Kluszewski and former Yankee Bob Cerv hit home runs. The Angels beat the Orioles 7–2.

The Angels lost their next eight games. But they were much better than expected. The team went 45–44 to end the season. It finished eighth in the AL, ahead of two other teams. The Angels had a 70–91 record. It remains the best record by a first-year expansion team in major league history.

THINK ABOUT IT

Expansion teams have to start from scratch. If you were starting a team, would you focus on getting young players who might struggle early but have long-term potential? Or would you build your team with veteran players who are established but nearing the end of their careers? Use examples from the book to explain your answer.

3

JIM FREGOSI SHINES FIRST

Angels fans didn't have much to cheer for in the 1960s. The team finished no better than fifth in the AL from 1963 to 1968. Yet during that time, Jim Fregosi became a fan favorite.

Fregosi was the Angels' first star. He was a slick-fielding shortstop and solid hitter. He played 11 seasons for the Angels. Fregosi made the All-Star Game in six of them. Owner Gene Autry always said Fregosi was his favorite player.

Fregosi joined the Angels as a 19-year-old rookie in 1961. By 1964, he was an All-Star. That season, he hit .277 with 18 home runs and 72 runs batted in (RBIs). In 1967, he won a Gold Glove for fielding excellence. In 1968, he led the AL in triples with 13. The Angels traded Fregosi to the New York Mets after the 1971 season. At the time, he held almost every team offensive record.

After retiring as a player, Fregosi managed the Angels. He led them to the AL West title in 1979. It was their first championship. The clinching game was special for Fregosi and Autry.

2

Times Jim Fregosi hit for the cycle, getting a single, double, triple, and home run in the same game.

- He did it in 1964 and 1968.
- He's the only Angels player to have done it twice.
- The Angels traded Fregosi for talented pitcher Nolan Ryan.

"I'll never forget Gene's eyes when I saw him after the game," Fregosi said. "It was as if a black cloud had been lifted from his head forever."

In 1998, the Angels retired Fregosi's No. 11 jersey. Don Baylor, a star of the 1979 team, said it was a fitting honor. "He had 'Angels' written on his chest, his forehead, everywhere," Baylor said.

The Angels' Jim Fregosi

4

NOLAN RYAN BECOMES THE STRIKEOUT KING

The Angels traded for New York Mets pitcher Nolan Ryan in December 1971. Ryan had all the raw skills. He threw harder than anyone in baseball. His fastball was clocked at more than 100 miles per hour (160 km/h). But he came with a question mark. In five seasons, his win/loss record was just 29–38. In his final season in New York, he had walked 116 batters in 152 innings.

However, almost as soon as he put on an Angels uniform,

Nolan Ryan pitches in the 1979 All-Star Game.

the 25-year-old Ryan changed. He became one of the baseball's most dominating pitchers. The question mark was erased. As an Angel, he still walked the most batters in the league six times. But he also struck out the most batters seven times.

Working with pitching coach Tom Morgan, Ryan made some changes in his delivery. He learned how to control his big curveball. He could throw strikes when he was in a jam. During the next eight seasons, Ryan won 138 games and threw four no-hitters. That tied the major league record. In 1973, Ryan struck out 383 batters—a major league record.

The Angels went to the postseason just once during Ryan's time in Anaheim. But he was one of baseball's most exciting players.

THE ULTIMATE TEST

Nolan Ryan's pitches often left the best hitters swinging at air. Still, Oakland Athletics slugger Reggie Jackson liked the challenge. "I love to bat against Nolan Ryan and I hate to bat against Nolan Ryan," Jackson said. "It's like ice cream. You may love it, but you don't want it shoveled down your throat by the gallon. I've never been afraid at the plate, but Mr. Ryan makes me uncomfortable."

5,714

Nolan Ryan's major league-record strikeout total.

- That is 839 more than second-place Randy Johnson.
- Ryan also holds the MLB record for walks with 2,795.
- He left the Angels after the 1979 season and played until 1993 with the Houston Astros and the Texas Rangers.

5 ANGELS FANS SAY "YES WE CAN!"

After the 1978 season, the Angels had reason for hope. They had finished second in the seven-team AL West and won 87 games. It was a team record for victories. In the offseason, the team made two trades with the Minnesota Twins. Star first baseman Rod Carew and outfielder "Disco" Danny Ford came to California.

The additions gave manager Jim Fregosi a strong lineup. The lineup also included power-hitting second baseman Bobby Grich, left fielder Don Baylor, and young first baseman and designated hitter Willie Mays Aikens. The pitching staff was solid, too. It had starters Nolan Ryan, Frank Tanana, and Dave Frost.

Danny Ford celebrates the Angels' first division title in 1979.

By the end of April, the Angels were in first place. It became clear this team would be special. Fans in Anaheim all season chanted "Yes We Can!" to support their team.

Don Baylor welcomes Danny Ford at home plate after a home run in the 1979 playoffs.

Six Angels were selected for the All-Star Game. In September, the Angels went 16–11 to clinch the division. Although the team lost in the AL Championship Series (ALCS), it was still a season for Angels fans to savor. It also opened the door for two more trips to the playoffs in the next seven years.

CALL HIM "GROOVE"

The Angels' biggest star in 1979 was Don Baylor. Nicknamed "Groove" for the way he got hot for a long time, Baylor had the season of his life. He hit .296 with 36 home runs. He also led the AL with 139 RBIs and 120 runs scored. He was named the AL Most Valuable Player (MVP).

2,908

Games the Angels played over 19 seasons before their first division championship season.

- Catcher Brian Downing had a team-high .326 batting average in 1979.
- Rod Carew and Nolan Ryan from the 1979 team went on to the Baseball Hall of Fame.

6

COLOR THE ANGELS RED

Today when the Angels play at home, Angel Stadium is covered in red. Red is the main color of the team's uniforms. Fans who come to games wear red shirts and red team caps. But it hasn't always been that way.

The Angels' Jim Edmonds hits a home run in a 1997 game.

The team has changed its uniform, caps, and logo several times. Even the team's name has changed. It began as the Los Angeles Angels in 1961. It became the California Angels from 1966 to 1996. From 1997 to 2004, the team was known as the Anaheim Angels. And since 2005, it has been called the Los Angeles Angels of Anaheim.

The team cap in the 1960s had a silver circle stitched around the top. That represented an angel's halo. Those caps gave birth to the team's nickname: the Halos.

From 1997 to 2001, the uniforms changed a lot. Under the ownership of Disney, the jerseys also had pinstripes and dark blue sleeves. A white angel's wing sprouted from a red A in "Angels" written across the chest. The cap featured the same winged A. The uniforms also featured a light blue color called periwinkle. Many players and fans disliked the uniforms. By coincidence, the team had several poor seasons in them.

In 2002, the Angels adopted their new red uniforms. The players loved them. So did fans. As pitcher Jarrod Washburn said after the Angels lost their season opener, "At least we got new uniforms."

Angels pitcher C. J. Wilson in 2012

6

Division championships the Angels won from 2002 through 2014, their first 13 seasons with red uniforms.

- The Angels also won their first and only World Series in 2002.
- The era of 2002 to 2004 was the team's greatest period of success.

THINK ABOUT IT

Do you believe the color of a team's uniforms can impact the way it plays? Write three or four sentences to explain your answer.

7

THE ANGELS HAVE A HEAVENLY SEASON IN 2002

The 2002 Anaheim Angels didn't look good to start the season. They won just six of their first 20 games. They were 10½ games out of first by April 26. But the Angels of 2002 could never be counted out. They went 88–49 over the final five months. That gave them 99 wins on the season. And 43 of those victories came after they trailed in a game.

"We were a late-inning comeback team," said Angels outfielder Tim Salmon.

Fans caught the fever. Every home game featured a sea of red, as fans clad in the Angels' new colors filled the seats. They loudly cheered one comeback victory after another.

The Angels celebrate winning the 2002 World Series.

SPIEZIO!

The Angels were eight outs from losing in Game 6 of the World Series. They trailed 5–0 when first baseman Scott Spiezio came to the plate. With two runners on, Spiezio hit a fly ball down the right-field line. It barely went over the short wall. The three-run home run started the Angels on a 6–5 comeback win. No team facing World Series elimination had ever overcome a five-run deficit. "I knew this team," Spiezio said. "All it needs is a little spark."

.611

Winning percentage for the 2002 Angels—the best in team history at the time.

- The Angels' Troy Glaus was named World Series MVP.
- Glaus batted .385 with three home runs and eight RBIs in seven World Series games.

It was an exciting team managed by Mike Scioscia. The Angels led the league with 1,603 hits and a .282 batting average. Six players hit 10 or more home runs. Third baseman Troy Glaus had 30. Garret Anderson hit 29 home runs and Salmon added 22.

Anaheim clinched the wild-card playoff spot. "That team was such a blue-collar team," Salmon said. "It was one game at a time, one day at a time, one pitch at a time."

That also was true in the postseason. The Angels lost their first game to the New York Yankees in the first round of the playoffs. Then the Angels won the series.

They did the same thing in the ALCS. The Angels beat the Minnesota Twins to earn the team's first AL pennant.

In the World Series, the Angels fell behind the San Francisco Giants three games to two. But they won Games 6 and 7 to win it all. In their 42nd season, the Angels finally were the champions of baseball.

8

"IRON MIKE" LEADS THE WAY

The Angels finished 70–92 in 1999. They hadn't been to the playoffs since 1986. So the team decided it was time to look for a new manager.

Angels general manager Bill Stoneman offered the job to Mike Scioscia. He had been an All-Star catcher for the Los Angeles Dodgers. Just 40 years old, Scioscia had been managing the Dodgers' top minor league team in Albuquerque, New Mexico. Before that, he'd been a bench coach for the Dodgers.

Mike Scioscia tips his hat to the crowd at a 2012 game.

19

Managers for the Angels between 1961 and 1999 before Scioscia was hired.

- Bill Rigney (1961–1969) had the most wins of any Angels manager before Scioscia, going 625–707.
- After the 2014 season, Scioscia had a record of 1,331–1,099.
- Scioscia had 11 winning seasons in his first 15.

To Stoneman, Scioscia seemed perfect for the job.

He'd been a tough player, known as "Iron Mike." Scioscia also knew pitching. He caught and worked with Dodgers pitchers on two World Series championship teams. Stoneman liked Scioscia's ability to communicate, his fairness, and his baseball knowledge. "He's a fellow we hope can help us get an Angels World Series ring," Stoneman said.

Scioscia did just that. He accepted the job for the 2000 season. And in his third season in 2002, the Angels won their first World Series.

THINK ABOUT IT

How important do you think a manager is to a baseball team? What qualities do you think make for a good manager?

Scioscia became a fixture in Anaheim. He helped build a steady, winning team. Over the next 12 years, Scioscia's teams won six AL West titles. By 2014, Scioscia had become the longest-serving manager in the majors. He's managed more seasons and won more games than any manager in Angels history. Scioscia's teams have emphasized aggressive base running, strong pitching, and fundamentals.

"One hundred percent, Scioscia is one of the best managers in the game," said former Angels outfielder Torii Hunter. "I played for him for five years, and I watched him look at baseball like he had the manual."

9

MONKEY BUSINESS COMES TO ANAHEIM

Officially, the Rally Monkey never has won a game for the Angels. He never has hit a home run or made an opposing outfielder slip on a banana peel.

Yet the monkey has been a part of the most successful era in Angels history. He's been a fan favorite at Angel Stadium since 2000. The Angels won their only World Series in 2002 when the monkey was a good-luck charm.

Angels fans bring their stuffed Rally Monkeys to games for good luck. If their team is tied or trailing late in a game, they wait for his appearance on the stadium's giant scoreboard. They cheer the video of the monkey jumping up and down alongside a flashing "Rally Time!" message. The

24

Times the Angels won games in 2002 after being tied or behind in the late innings when the Rally Monkey appeared.

- The clip came from the movie *Ace Ventura: Pet Detective.*
- The Angels scored two runs in the ninth inning to beat the San Francisco Giants 6–5 in the Rally Monkey's debut.

THINK ABOUT IT

Do you believe in the power of the Rally Monkey? Is it just a coincidence that the Angels have won so many games after he appears? Write three or four sentences to explain your answer.

stadium gets louder as fans urge the Angels to score.

"It's kind of a signal," said Peter Bull, an Angels executive. "It's kind of a belief that the Angels can come back in any situation. So that gets the fans into the game to scream more than they normally would, to provide more positive energy."

The Rally Monkey was a happy accident. On June 6, 2000, the Angels were trailing late in a game. The video operator decided to run a video of a monkey jumping up and down. It was just one of many video clips the team had used that year. This time, however, "Rally Monkey" appeared on the screen with it. The Angels rallied to win the game. When the Angels trailed the next night, the monkey made another appearance. The team again rallied to win. Suddenly, the monkey was a hit.

An Angels fan holds up a Rally Monkey during a 2012 game.

10

TROUT MAKES A SPLASH

Almost a year before Mike Trout played his first big-league game, Angels manager Mike Scioscia said he would be a star. It was the summer of 2010. Trout was just a year out of high school. He was playing in Class A, a long way from the majors. But Scioscia had seen Trout run, hit, and field. He raved about Trout's power and speed. Scioscia also said Trout's personality was suited for success.

"He's got the makeup," Scioscia said. "He's focused. He's just a player with as much upside as any player that has put on the uniform."

After a short time with the team in 2011, Trout was ready for stardom in 2012. Trout had one of the best rookie seasons of all time. He hit .326 with 30 home runs. Plus he led the AL in runs scored and stolen bases. In the outfield, Trout jumped above the fence to rob four opponents of home runs. He was unanimously voted AL Rookie of the Year. He finished second in voting for the AL MVP Award.

At Angel Stadium, a portion of the seats in left field were designated

Mike Trout hits a home run in a 2015 game.

the "Trout Farm." Fans in the section wear special Angels caps. The caps have replica trout tails and heads at the back and front. The fans also hold up signs with Trout's name and picture.

In 2013, Trout hit .323 with 27 home runs. He led the league in runs and walks. He again finished second in the MVP voting. In 2014, Trout won the AL MVP Award at age 23 after hitting a career-best 36 home runs. He helped the Angels win the AL West. Only four other MVPs had ever been younger.

Trout will be an Angel for a long time. Before the 2014 season, he signed a $144.5 million deal to play for the Angels through 2020.

Mike Trout makes a catch during a 2014 game.

24

Players selected before Mike Trout in the first round of the 2009 MLB Draft.

- At 21 years and 58 days old, Trout became the youngest AL Rookie of the Year.
- He made his fourth All-Star Game in 2015.

LIKE A METEOR

Mike Trout also played basketball and football at his high school in Millville, New Jersey. As a 6-foot-1 forward, he could dunk a basketball from a standing start.

11

THE "BIG A" STILL SHINES

In their first five seasons, the Angels were a team without a true home. Wrigley Field in Los Angeles was their first ballpark in 1961. It had been built in 1925. But it was too small. There were only 20,500 seats. The fences were so close that players hit 248 home runs there that season. That was an MLB record. For the next four seasons, the Angels played at Dodger Stadium. They had to share the ballpark with the Los Angeles Dodgers.

The Angels finally got their own home in 1966. That season, the team moved to Anaheim. It began play in brand-new Anaheim Stadium. The ballpark was built for $24 million on 157 acres (0.4 hectares). The area previously had been farmland.

The stadium, now called Angel Stadium of Anaheim, was a beautiful ballpark. Fans could look out over the outfield fences to the wide-open fields and San Gabriel Mountains.

Giant hats greet fans outside Angel Stadium of Anaheim.

A tall, A-shaped scoreboard in left field led fans and media to call the stadium the "Big A."

Angel Stadium of Anaheim

The ballpark was changed drastically in 1979 and 1980. That's when it also became home to the Los Angeles Rams football team. At that time, the outfield views disappeared. The stadium was enclosed. More than 20,000 seats were added beyond the outfield fences.

When the Rams moved to St. Louis after the 1994 season, the facility was remodeled. Today it again has the open views beyond the outfield. In addition, the $100 million project upgraded seating, walkways, and restaurants.

The famous giant Angels hats were added in front of the main ballpark entrance. Terraced bullpens in left field also were added. And beyond center field, an artificial waterfall over giant rocks gave the park a unique look.

3

Major league parks older than Angel Stadium of Anaheim.

- Fenway Park in Boston opened in 1912.
- Wrigley Field, home of the Chicago Cubs, opened in 1914.
- Dodger Stadium in Los Angeles opened in 1962.

12 LIGHTS, CAMERA . . . PLAY BALL!

It seems only fitting that a baseball team located near Hollywood and founded by a movie star should be in the movies. Team owner Gene Autry had been in more than 90 films as a singing cowboy. The Angels also have had a starring role in several movies.

The biggest was Disney's *Angels in the Outfield*, made in 1994. In it, a boy in a foster home gets his father to promise he'll straighten out his

An *Angels in the Outfield* DVD

1

Actual former Angels player who had a role in *Angels in the Outfield.*

- Third baseman Carney Lansford had retired two years earlier.
- Former Angels outfielder Reggie Jackson was in *The Naked Gun.*

life if the Angels win the pennant. The boy is a big fan of the team. But he knows he'll need a miracle because the Angels are horrible. So he prays for help. An angel gets involved to help the team become a winner.

There was one funny twist to the movie. It was filmed in Oakland, not in Anaheim. At the time of filming, the Angels' stadium was in use by the Los Angeles Rams. Six years later, Disney made a sequel called *Angels in the Infield*. It was filmed in Toronto.

In 1988, the Angels were part of the plot of *The Naked Gun*. It is a comedy about a bungling police officer. He tries to foil a crime at an Angels game.

Other films about the Angels include *Taking Care of Business* from 1990. In that one, the Angels play the Chicago Cubs in the World Series. The 1991 movie *Talent for the Game* is about an Angels scout. And in 2002, the movie *Air Bud: Seventh Inning Fetch* featured a golden retriever named Buddy. He's such a good player that he gets to play for the Angels.

THE ANGELS' OWN FILM

Before every game, the Angels show a short film of past highlights and stars on the giant scoreboard. It's accompanied by the song "Calling All Angels" by the rock group Train.

12 KEY DATES

1961
The Los Angeles Angels begin play as an expansion team in the AL.

1964
Angels pitcher Dean Chance wins the Cy Young Award with a 20–9 record and 1.65 earned-run average.

1966
The team moves from Los Angeles to Anaheim and becomes the California Angels.

1970
Alex Johnson wins the AL batting title on the final day of the season, finishing with a .329 average. He's the only Angels player to have won a batting championship.

1973
Nolan Ryan throws the first of his four no-hitters with the Angels—a 3–0 victory over the Kansas City Royals on May 15.

1979
The Angels beat the Kansas City Royals on September 25 to clinch their first division title.

1984
The Angels' Mike Witt becomes the 11th pitcher ever to throw a perfect game, beating the Texas Rangers on September 30.

1986
The Angels come within one out of going to their first World Series but lose 7–6 to the Red Sox in 11 innings in Game 5 of the ALCS. The Angels then lose Games 6 and 7 as well.

1998

The Angels play their first season in their remodeled home ballpark, renamed Edison International Field. Today it is called Angel Stadium of Anaheim.

2002

Reliever Troy Percival gets the final out of a 4–1 victory over the San Francisco Giants to clinch the Angels' first World Series championship on October 27.

2004

In his first season with the Angels, outfielder Vladimir Guerrero hits .337 with 39 home runs and 126 RBIs to win AL MVP honors.

2011

Mike Trout makes his major league debut, going 0-for-3 against the Seattle Mariners on July 8. A year later, he is named AL Rookie of the Year after his first full season.

GLOSSARY

designated hitter
In the AL, teams may select a batter to hit in the lineup in place of the pitcher.

draft
A system by which leagues spread new talent among all the teams. Teams select new players in order based on the worst to best finish the previous season.

expansion team
A team added to an existing league.

free agent
A player who is not signed with a team and is free to join any team.

pennant
A league championship.

retire
To end one's career. Teams can also retire a player's or coach's number as a tribute so that no future member of that team can wear the number.

rookie
A first-year player in a league.

unanimously
Done in total agreement.

veteran
A player with a lot of experience.

wild-card
Playoff spots given to the best teams that did not win their respective division.

FOR MORE INFORMATION

Books

Donovan, Pete. *Under the Halo: The Official History of Angels Baseball.* San Rafael, CA: Insight Editions, 2012.

George-Warren, Holly. *Public Cowboy No. 1: The Life and Times of Gene Autry.* New York: Oxford University Press, 2007.

Goldman, Rob. *Nolan Ryan: The Making of a Pitcher.* Chicago: Triumph Books, 2014.

Websites

Baseball Reference

www.baseball-reference.com

Los Angeles Angels

losangeles.angels.mlb.com

National Baseball Hall of Fame

www.baseballhall.org

INDEX

About the Author

Doug Williams is a freelance writer in San Diego. He is a former newspaper reporter and editor. He's written several books about sports and writes for many national and San Diego-area publications. He is a lifelong baseball fan.